PERIMETER

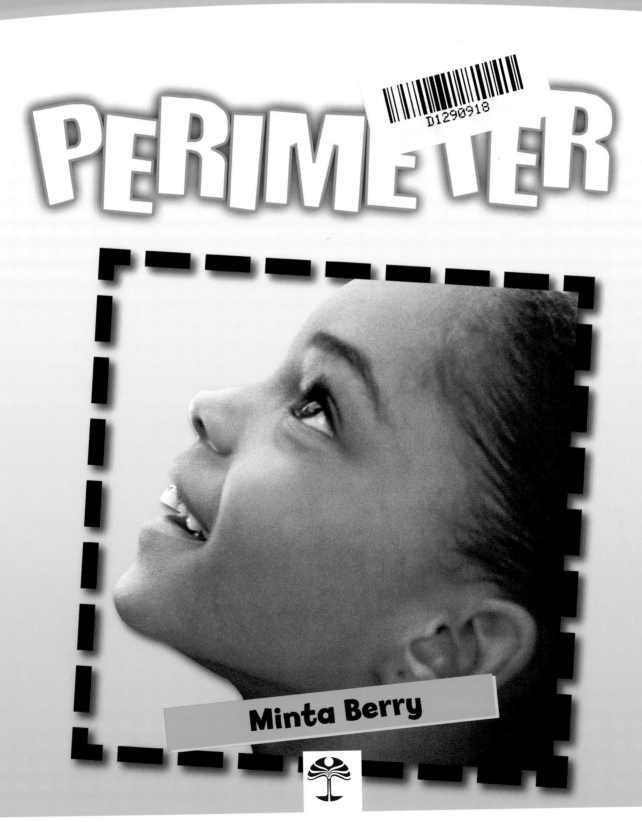

Minta Berry

Crabtree Publishing Company

www.crabtreebooks.com

Author: Minta Berry
Publishing plan research and development:
   Sean Charlebois, Reagan Miller
   Crabtree Publishing Company
Editor: Reagan Miller
Proofreader: Crystal Sikkens
Cover design: Margaret Amy Salter
Editorial director: Kathy Middleton
Production coordinator: Margaret Amy Salter
Prepress technician: Margaret Amy Salter
Print coordinator: Katherine Berti
Project manager: Kirsten Holm, Shivi Sharma (Planman
   Technologies)
Photo research: Iti Shrotriya (Planman Technologies)
Technical art: Arka Roy Chaudhary (Planman Technologies)

Photographs:

Cover: ivanastar/iStockPhoto (pool), Shutterstock (br); P4: BMCL/
Shutterstock; P5: (bkgd) Thank You/Shutterstock, (fgd) Andy
Dean Photography/Shutterstock; P6: Elena Elisseeva/Shutterstock;
P7: (t bkgd) Moonbeam/Shutterstock, (t fgd) Elena Elisseeva/
Shutterstock, (b) Karam Miri/123RF; P9: Robin Thorn; P11: Rainer/
Dreamstime.com; P12: (t) John T Takai/Shutterstock, (b) Josep M
Penalver Rufas/Shutterstock; P15: James Camp | Dreamstime.com;
P17: (t) Christopher Oates/Shutterstock, (b) Christopher
Oates/Shutterstock.
(t = top, b = bottom, l = left, c= center, r = right, bkgd =
background, fgd = foreground)

Library and Archives Canada Cataloguing in Publication

Berry, Minta
      Perimeter / Minta Berry.

(My path to math)
Includes index.
Issued also in electronic formats.
ISBN 978-0-7787-5276-9 (bound).--ISBN 978-0-7787-5265-3 (pbk.)

      1. Perimeters (Geometry)--Juvenile literature. I. Title. II. Series: My
path to math

QA465.B47 2011   j516   C2011-906796-X

Library of Congress Cataloging-in-Publication Data

Berry, Minta.
   Perimeter / Minta Berry.
      p. cm. -- (My path to math)
   Includes index.
   ISBN 978-0-7787-5276-9 (reinforced library binding : alk. paper) -- ISBN 978-
0-7787-5265-3 (pbk. : alk. paper) -- ISBN 978-1-4271-8806-9 (electronic pdf) --
ISBN 978-1-4271-9647-7 (electronic html)
   1. Measurement--Juvenile literature. 2. Area measurement--Juvenile
literature. 3. Perimeters (Geometry)--Juvenile literature. I. Title.
   QA465.B47 2012
   516'.152--dc23
                                          2011040398

Crabtree Publishing Company

www.crabtreebooks.com   1-800-387-7650

Printed in the U.S.A./012014/SN20131105

Published in Canada
Crabtree Publishing
616 Welland Ave.
St. Catharines, ON
L2M 5V6

Published in the United States
Crabtree Publishing
PMB 59051
350 Fifth Avenue, 59th Floor
New York, New York 10118

Published in the United Kingdom
Crabtree Publishing
Maritime House
Basin Road North, Hove
BN41 1WR

Published in Australia
Crabtree Publishing
3 Charles Street
Coburg North
VIC 3058

Contents

Exploring Perimeter

The Vargas family is moving to a new house. Martin and Ramon will share a large room. They want to know how big their room will be.

Ramon gets a ball of string. The boys stretch the string around the edge of their new room. They are measuring the **perimeter** of the room. The perimeter is the distance around any figure.

Activity Box

Place paper clips end to end around the perimeter of this book. How many paper clips does it take to measure the perimeter?

The Vargas family's new home is larger than their old home. They will have more space now.

Using Objects to Measure Perimeter

Cari hopes her favorite rug will fit in her new room. She decides to use her feet to measure the perimeter of her new room. Then she will measure the perimeter of her rug and compare them.

She walks heel to toe down one wall of the room. She counts 16 feet. She turns the corner and starts down the next wall. She keeps counting as she walks. Cari finds that it takes about 70 of her feet to walk around the perimeter of her new room.

Activity Box

Choose an object in the room you are sitting in. Use your feet to measure the distance around the object. How many feet did you count as you measured the perimeter?

Cari uses her heel-to-toe method to measure the perimeter of many objects.

Cari goes back to her old house. She uses her feet to measure the perimeter of the rug in her bedroom.

Cari finds that it takes about 50 of her feet to walk around the perimeter of her rug.

The perimeter of her new room is about 70 feet. The perimeter of her rug is about 50 feet. Will her rug fit in her new room?

Yes, the rug will fit in Cari's new room since the perimeter of the room is larger than the perimeter of the rug.

Using a Grid to Measure Perimeter

There is a pool in the back yard of the new home. Ramon and Martin see a **grid** on the pool cover. A **grid** is a pattern of **squares** made by lines spaced evenly apart. Ramon says that if they count the squares on the grid as they walk around the pool they will know the pool's perimeter.

1 2 3 4 5 6 7...

Activity Box

Look at the grid above. Use it to find the perimeter around the pool. What is the perimeter of the Vargas family's pool?

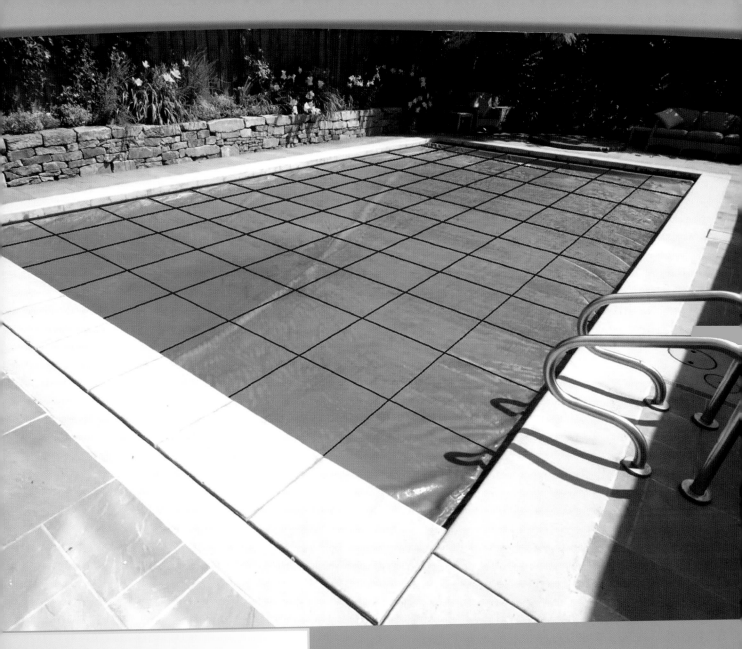

The grid on a pool cover can be used to find the perimeter of the pool.

Estimating Perimeter

Ramon and his mother work together to plan the family's new garden. Ramon's mother helps him draw the shape of their new flowerbeds on grid paper.

Vargas Family Garden

One flowerbed has five sides.

Ramon uses the drawings to **estimate** the perimeter of each flowerbed. To estimate means to find out about how many or how much. He counts each square or part of a square on the grid paper as one unit.

Because Ramon included even part squares when counting, his measurement is an estimation rather than an exact measurement. He estimates the perimeter of one flowerbed is 12 units.

10

Finding the perimeter helps a gardener plan how many plants will fit in each garden bed.

Activity Box

Look at the grid below. What is the estimated perimeter of this flowerbed?

Vargas Family Garden

Measuring Perimeter

Cari and her friend Macie measure the length of the walls in the rooms of the new house. Then they make drawings of the rooms. They write their measurements on their drawings.

The yardstick is divided into feet (ft) and inches (in).

Cari uses a **meterstick** to measure the rooms. A **meterstick** is a tool used to measure length. A **meterstick** is one meter (m) long. Cari measures some of the rooms in meters.

The meterstick is divided into centimeters (cm) and millimeters (mm).

Macie uses a **yardstick** to measure the rooms. A yardstick is also a tool used to measure length. A yardstick measures length in feet and inches. She measures some of the rooms in feet.

Activity Box

Measure the **triangle** and the **rectangle** using a ruler. How long is each side of the triangle? How long is each side of the rectangle?

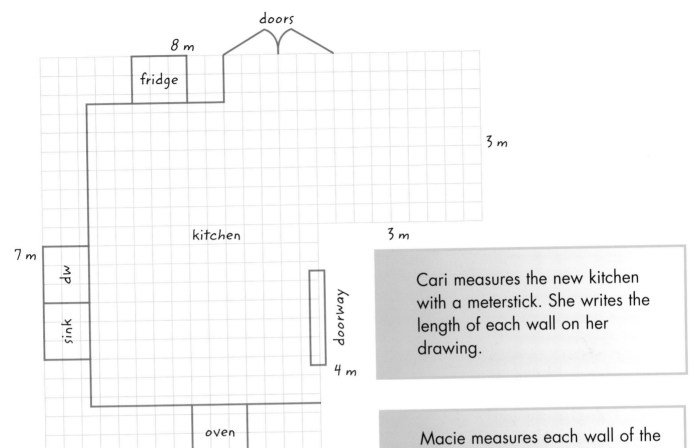

doors

8 m

fridge

3 m

kitchen

3 m

7 m

dw

sink

doorway

4 m

Cari measures the new kitchen with a meterstick. She writes the length of each wall on her drawing.

oven

5 m

Macie measures each wall of the living room with a yardstick. She includes the width of the window.

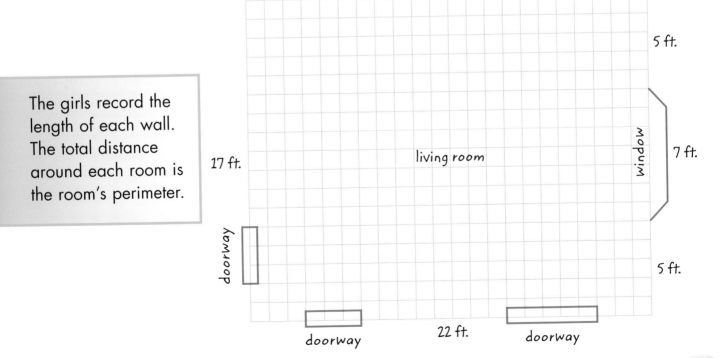

22 ft.

5 ft.

The girls record the length of each wall. The total distance around each room is the room's perimeter.

17 ft.

living room

window

7 ft.

doorway

5 ft.

doorway

22 ft.

doorway

Finding Perimeter Using Addition

Mr. Vargas plans to put a fence around the yard. He carefully marks the **boundary** of the yard. The boundary is a line along the edge of the Vargas family's land.

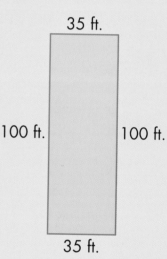

Ramon and Martin use a tape measure to find the length of each side of the yard. Ramon writes down the length of each side as he measures. He finds the perimeter by adding the length of each side.

100 ft. + 100 ft. + 35 ft. + 35 ft. = 270 ft.

The perimeter of the yard is 270 feet.

The yard is 100 ft. + 100 ft. + 35 ft. + 35 ft. = 270 ft. Mr. Vargas needs 270 feet of fencing.

Activity Box

What is the perimeter of each shape?

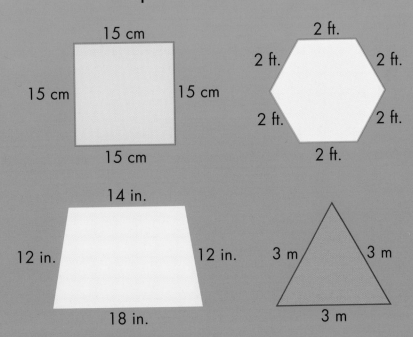

15 cm

15 cm | 15 cm

15 cm

2 ft.

2 ft. | 2 ft.

2 ft. | 2 ft.

2 ft.

14 in.

12 in. | 12 in.

18 in.

3 m | 3 m

3 m

Finding Perimeter Using Multiplication

Ramon wants to build a doghouse in the shape of a rectangle. A **rectangle** has four sides. The opposite sides of a rectangle are equal in length.

Cari shows Ramon a **formula** for figuring out the perimeter of a rectangle. A formula is a set of symbols that expresses a mathematical rule. Cari writes down the formula:

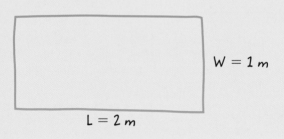

W = 1 m

L = 2 m

2 times the length + 2 times the width = the perimeter of a rectangle

$(2 \times 2m) + (2 \times 1m) = 6m$

Activity Box

Use the formula to find the perimeter for each rectangle.

W = 1 cm.

L = 3 cm.

W = 2 in

L = 5 in.

Mr. Vargas lays a new floor in the kitchen of their new home. He uses square tiles. A **square** is a shape with four equal sides.

Before he begins, Mr. Vargas needs to find the perimeter of one tile. He tells Ramon that the formula to find the perimeter of the square tile is 4s. He tells Ramon that the "s" stands for "sides."

Because all four sides are the same length, he can multiply the length of one side by four. The formula means 4 times the length of one side.

Ramon measures a floor tile. One side of the tile measures 12 inches. Use the formula 4s to help Ramon find the perimeter of the square tile.

$s = 12$ in.

What is the perimeter of one tile?

4×12 in. $= 48$ in.

Drawing Figures

Ramon and Martin draw the perimeter of a rug on grid paper using **linear units**. A **linear unit** is a unit used to measure length. The boys have measured things in centimeters and meters. They have also measured things in yards, feet, and inches.

Each square of the grid paper can be used to show one linear unit. Martin shows the **dimensions**, or measurement of length in each direction, of a rug.

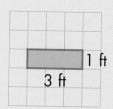

The rug is three feet long and one foot wide.

Activity Box

Draw these shapes on a piece of grid paper. Use the dimensions given below.

1. Draw a rectangle that is 8 feet long and 3 feet wide.

2. Draw a triangle that is 4 cm on each side.

Mrs. Vargas will grow tomatoes in the new garden. She wants to keep the plants safe from rabbits. She buys a roll of fence. The roll is 20 feet long.

She asks Ramon to draw a tomato bed that would use the whole roll with no fence material left over. Ramon drew several shapes for the tomato bed.

Which of these beds would use the 20 feet of fencing? Which would need more than 20 feet?

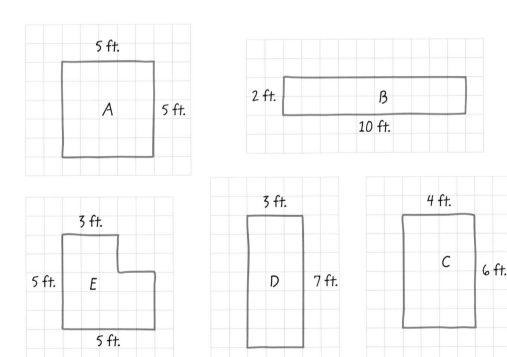

Drawing a Plan

Cari's friend Macie learns that her family is going to build a new house. Macie and Cari decide to draw a floor plan of her new home.

The house will be 14 m wide and 12 m long. The garage will extend on the left side. It will measure 7 meters by 6 meters.

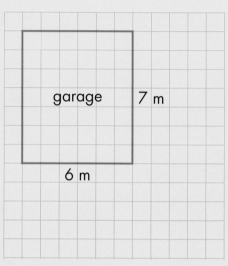

Macie starts to get an idea of the dimensions of her new house.

Activity Box

If you were going to build your own house what would you design?

- Think about the rooms your family would need.

- How big would those rooms need to be?

- Think about what activities you like. How much space would you want for those activities?

Use a piece of grid paper to design the house of your dreams. Include measurements for each room.

Hint: Find the perimeter of rooms in your home so you have an idea of the measurements for your dream home plan.

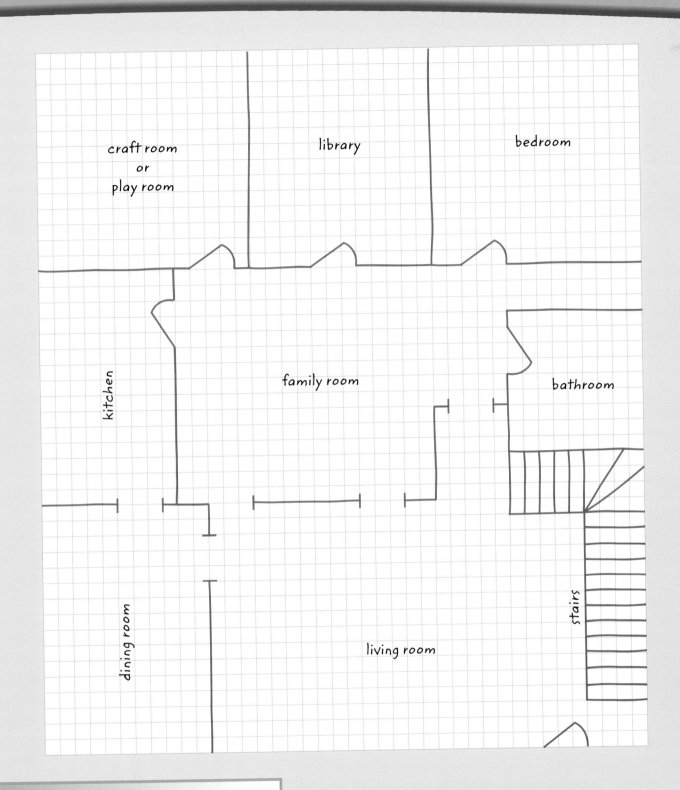

craft room
or
play room

library

bedroom

kitchen

family room

bathroom

dining room

living room

stairs

A floor plan shows the dimensions of each room of the house. Each square of the grid paper is equal to one foot.

Glossary

boundary A line that determines the limits of a shape

dimension Measurement of length in each direction

estimate To find out about how much or how many

formula A set of symbols that expresses a mathematical rule

grid A pattern of horizontal and vertical lines

linear unit Any measure of length (yards, feet, inches, meters, centimeters)

meterstick A tool that is one meter long and used to measure length

perimeter The distance around any figure

rectangle A four-sided shape whose angles form right angles and whose opposite sides are of equal length

square A shape with four equal sides and with right angles at all four corners

triangle A shape with three straight sides and three corners

yardstick A tool used to measure length in feet and inches

Perimeter Facts

Shape	Example	Find Perimeter
triangle	3 cm 3 cm 3 cm	Add the length of each side 3 cm + 3 cm + 3 cm = 9 cm
rectangle	W = 2 in. L = 6 in.	Add the length of each side 6 in. + 6 in. + 2 in. + 2 in. = 16 in. Or, use the formula 2L + 2W (2 × 6 in.) + (2 × 2 in.) = 16 in.
square	s = 5 cm	Add the length of each side 5 cm + 5 cm + 5 cm + 5 cm = 20 cm Or, use the formula 4s 4 × 5 cm = 20 cm
other polygons	2 in. 3 in. 3 in. 4 in.	Add the length of each side 2 in. + 3 in. + 4 in. + 3 in. = 12 in.

Index